THROUGH IT ALL

God Still Gave Me Favor

WANDA R. BRIGHT

ISBN 978-1-0980-6098-5 (paperback)
ISBN 978-1-0980-6099-2 (digital)

Copyright © 2020 by Wanda R. Bright

All rights reserved. No part of this publication may be reproduced, distributed, or transmitted in any form or by any means, including photocopying, recording, or other electronic or mechanical methods without the prior written permission of the publisher. For permission requests, solicit the publisher via the address below.

Christian Faith Publishing, Inc.
832 Park Avenue
Meadville, PA 16335
www.christianfaithpublishing.com

Printed in the United States of America

This book is dedicated to my grandparents who raised me and showed me the way to righteousness, Elder Kermit N. Haynes and Mother Ann M. Haynes. If it wasn't for them giving me this firm foundation, I don't know where I would be right now. Probably not leaning on Jesus to carry me through the situations I have been through.

To my parents, Ronald K. Haynes and Doris B. Haynes, for their continued love and support and for always wanting me to be their third wheel. I don't know what they will do without me or vice versa.

To my beloved and supportive husband, James R. Bright, Jr., who always wants all my free time and then some. You've got to love him!

ACKNOWLEDGMENT

I would like to first thank my almighty Savior for being the author and the finisher of my soul and for giving me the push to do this. A special thank you to my husband for giving me the time and space to do this project. Thank you to my pastor and my church family at First United Church of Jesus Christ (Apostolic), a.k.a. The Church of Champions for their continued prayers, especially my prayer partners. I also want to thank my best friends for hanging in there with me from the beginning and my sorority sisters who has given me that extra push. They know who they are.

CONTENTS

Introduction 9
Chapter 1: Teenage Years 13
Chapter 2: God's Healing Power 17
Chapter 3: Non-Motherhood 30
Chapter 4: Career Life 37
Chapter 5: The Dating Game and Marriage 45

INTRODUCTION

This book is for those who need more faith in their lives. It's for those who need to know that it's okay to lean on God for help. This book is about my life struggles and how God's love and mercy has lifted me up every time from whatever I was going through or helped me to get to a higher level in Christ and in life (i.e. my jobs, my health, my family, marriage, etc.). Let me help you get closer to Christ, have a better relationship with him, and not give up on yourself.

    I wrote this with the intention to help people heal and for me to heal and become a better person as well. I also wrote this with the intention for you and me to live the life God wants us to live, which is to live for him. I want people to know that we have a Savior to lean on, when times get rough, when the going gets tough. I want people to know that it's okay to cry, it's okay to pray and lay prostrate before the Lord. It's okay to feel lonely. It's okay to not make a lot of money because God will supply all of our needs according to his riches in glory.

I want others to know that "this too shall pass." The Bible tells us that, "weeping may endure for a night, but joy comes in the morning." Through my story, you will see how joy comes in the morning, in every situation. It may not come when you want it to, but it comes right on time. It may not be your season, but your season will come. We just have to exercise patience in God. The Bible also tells us not to be anxious for nothing (Philippians 4:6). People are so antsy; they don't want to wait on God. They go out there, and do it themselves, and mess it up every time. Then people wonder why something isn't happening for them. This is because you are not abiding by the Word of the Lord, which is the Bible. Once we abide in his word and do what he tells us to do, God will supply all of your needs. You cannot walk this journey by yourself. You must walk with God. He is the author and the finisher of our faith. He is Alpha and Omega, the beginning and the end. He is the only wise God!

Times are hard and they're not going to get any easier. But if you put your faith and trust in God, those times get bearable and easy to manage with Christ on our side. You will see this throughout my story.

My favorite scripture is *"And let us not be weary in well doing; for in due season we shall reap, if we faint not" (Galatians 6:9).*

I live by this scripture. I try not to be weary in well doing in all situations. As I start feeling weary, something just reminds me that you need to keep going. That's the not fainting part of the scripture. If I keep going and doing what I'm supposed to do, I will reap that work in God's time, when he's ready to give it to me. This excites me to be rewarded by God. This is why I do what I do. Not to be confused with getting rewarded by man. Man is not going to get me into heaven, but my good deeds that I do from my heart and the work I do in my faith, because "faith without works is dead" (James 2:17–26). As my pastor always says, "We must apply the Word!"

I pray that this book blesses you and that this will make you seek a relationship with God, if you don't have one already. Also, I hope this will make you seek God first in everything that you do, before you do it. You must be obedient to the voice of God, but you cannot hear God's voice without going into his presence. Go into that prayer closet and pray until you get in his presence, stay there for a while, he may start talking to you. You just have to be open and receptive of him speaking to you. So, stay focused on him and what he has called you to do, as I do the same.

CHAPTER 1
Teenage Years

I was baptized "in the name of Jesus Christ" (Acts 2:38) at the early age of seven. I received the mighty power of the Holy Ghost (Acts 5:32) at the age of thirteen. Between those ages, I had the roughest time in school. Kids want to tease me; boys want to touch me inappropriately. Girls want to fight and bully me, because the boys liked me or I was a pretty girl. I was raped at the age of twelve, right before my thirteenth birthday. I was too embarrassed to go to school, but I had people who still loved and cared about me that they would walk me home from school to make sure I got home safely or my big play brothers who would stand near my house on surrounding blocks to beat up the guys who were responsible.

I never asked none of these people to do what they did, but God said, vengeance is mine (Romans 12:19). I went to God and said, "Why me, Lord?" I didn't do anything to deserve this. He didn't respond at that time. He was showing me he's here with me. This is when I said to myself, let me just pray and turn my life over to God. So that following Sunday, they made the altar call. I went up to get prayed for and said I want to be filled with the Holy Ghost speaking in tongues which is God's love language. I stayed on that altar until I did. How exciting and fulfilled I felt, riding on cloud nine. Nothing can steal this joy from me.

It didn't stop there. When I say I was bullied, I was bullied by one girl who was bigger than me from seventh until ninth grade. This bully would at least once a week take my lunch money from me, so I wasn't able to eat lunch some days. I was scared of this girl, because she was bigger than me and she fought and beat up girls and boys all the time, ever since elementary school. Since I have seen her do this in elementary school, this is what made me scared of her, but I was not scared of anyone else at school. She fought like a dude. One day the bully and her cousin were walking with me home along with some others, and a boy touched me inappropriately and I hit him back and he got mad and hit me back, so we started fighting and I whipped his tail from the top of the block to my house. The bully couldn't believe I could fight and was in disbelief, but was laughing so hard because I whipped a boy's tail! So my dad came out and wanted to know what was going on and the bully told my dad what happened and then said the boy's sister wanted to fight me because I beat up her brother. My dad asked, "Is this true?" She said, "Yes." My dad proceeded with, "Well, we can take this in the backyard to finish it." The girl was smart enough to say, "No, never mind, I'll just leave." God's love protected me from going any further.

Fast forward to near the end of the school year, the bully caught up with me at lunch and I was eating lunch at a friend's house. The bully wanted me to come to the sidewalk to fight her. My friends were like, "No, don't do it." I was like, "Yes, I have to because she will stop after today." I said, "God has not given me the spirit of fear; but of power, and of love, and of a sound mind (2 Timothy

1:7)." So I went on and stepped to the bully to fight. She said, "I won't fight you. I just wanted to see if you had the courage to step to me." Then went to say, "If anybody steps to you and I'm around, I got your back." See how God steps in and fight your battles (2 Chronicles 32:8).

Now, as I got into high school, some students were talking about me behind my back. Some students I became friends with or were just friends with them since elementary or junior high school. God gave me the courage to move on. Didn't have any problems since tenth grade. Then, at the end of twelfth grade, one of my classmates came to me and said, "Despite what has been said about you throughout the years, I know it not to be true. You are one of the sweetest and friendliest people I know. You are also strong." I told her, "I didn't even know you were paying me any attention and thank you for those kind words." She then told me to continue to be the person I am and don't let no one discourage me. I was like, "Lord, thank you for letting your light shine through me (Matthew 5:16)."

CHAPTER 2
God's Healing Power

At the age of nineteen, I was diagnosed with a blood disease that would never go away. This disease made me distance myself from having relationships with men. Thinking they would never want to date or marry me because of it. Even had myself scared to have children. This was the "fall on your knees and pray until something happens"-type of situation. So, I did fall on my knees and prayed to God because I didn't know who else to turn to but God.

Praise be to God, the next time I went to the doctor, which was a year later, I had one percent of the disease left in my bloodstream. Years later, I took a blood test and it was nowhere to be found. Not doubting that it was gone, I take a test every year and it is not in my blood any longer. Thanks be to God that I am healed by his stripes. It says in his word that by his stripes we are healed (Isaiah 53:5). Till this day I still thank God for his healing power.

At the age of thirty-six, I was diagnosed with hypertension/high blood pressure. This was two years after being in the master's program and trying to make ends meet. As I had just finished up my thesis for receiving my master's degree and had just defended the thesis, I went to my job and as lunch time was getting near, I starting feeling funny. My head felt like it was about to burst. Then that feeling went to my arms while I was eating lunch. I thought if I ate, it will go away but it didn't. So my supervisor at the time told me to go to the hospital.

I caught a cab over to Providence Hospital in D.C. They took several tests and took my blood pressure. It was so high that the emergency room employees said, "Thank God that you came when you did, any higher, you could have had a stroke." Thank God for my church family, sisters Lisa and Alicia, for coming to support me and take me home afterward. My parents never came to the hospital, but made sure that they were kept informed by talking to Lisa and Alicia. The hospital released me, prescribed some medicine, and sent me on my way, but I was still feeling bad. I felt bad for a whole week. That Friday night, we had a Good Friday service. My Bishop prayed for me that night and thanked God that I came despite of me feeling the way I did. He even said I still didn't look well but said, "I'm glad you came, because there is help in the sanctuary." I started coming back to normal, after this point.

Later on, I discovered that feeling I was having was a migraine. I could not be around light, I just wanted to lie down and be in the dark. I felt like I was going under. I continued to have those migraines, but had to learn to cope and manage them throughout the years. I had an MRI done and nothing was discovered to trigger the pain I was having. So, I had to learn to stop eating frozen meals with a sodium count over 600mg to not even eating frozen meals period! I had to stop eating processed meats; I was famous for buying processed meats to make sandwiches so I could take my lunch to work. Even eating anything with more than 400mg of sodium took a lot of discipline, but before I got to this point. I had another episode of that feeling I had at the age of thirty-six, I had it again at the age of forty-three. I was at work and told one of my co-workers that I will need for her to take me to the emergency room. She stayed with me the entire time I was in the ER. She kept my parents abreast of what was going on with me, after many hours of sitting and waiting to even get seen by someone in ER. This was the worst experience in a hospital ever.

They took my blood pressure, laid me on a gurney, the hooked be up to an IV. They started shooting me up with morphine, thinking that was going to take the pain away, but every time they shot me with morphine, I felt like I was having an out of body experience. I told my co-worker that it felt like the devil took over. Then they wanted to take a bone marrow of my spine or stick a needle in my spine and stand the chance of being paralyzed after that. I was like no way. They were like, "The CAT scan is coming back normal, so we want to make sure we are not missing anything." I was like, "I will go to my neurologists and have a MRI done again." They would not release me. So I released myself.

I called my co-worker and told her I had called my then boyfriend, now husband, to come to the hospital and he would have to take me home so my co-worker wouldn't have to. Then I told her to come to the back, so she can assist me on getting out of the hospital. They told my co-worker, "If she can go to the bathroom by herself, we will release her." I went to the bathroom by myself. They were taking too long for my release, so we just walked out and I told them to send the information that I needed to my e-mail. My co-worker was laughing, but was concerned all at the same time. She asked, "Are you sure you want to do this?" I said, "Girl, yes! God healed me before and he can do it again, without their expertise and help. Whose report will you believe in? I believe in the report of the Lord!" She drove me to the metro to pick up my then boyfriend, now husband, then took us to my car, so he could drive me home.

The next day, I contacted my neurologists and he examined me. He referred me to take yet another MRI. The MRI still could not find *anything*. Praise God! So from that day forward, I just had to start taking it easy, and stop stressing, and letting things out, and letting things go. I had to stop holding my feelings in and stop worrying about everything, as that was stressing me. I then learned that stress is the silent killer and had to come to the conclusion that I was *too blessed to be stressed*.

I have had migraines after that, and they did not completely go away until I left that job and environment. When I started a new job, I was less stressed and more relaxed. Even at the new job and location, if I felt stressed, I could always go out for lunch, take a walk, or sit outside relaxing and refreshing myself to get through the rest of the day. So when this particular job began to get too stressful and I started having migraines again, just not as bad because I already knew how to manage the stress, I still had to take myself out of that environment. As I learned, not to stay anywhere or in an environment that was hostile and stressful. I know that you will get stressed at work, but not to the point that it will make you sick. As that job will always be there, but you will not. Once you are gone, they will find someone else to fill your position.

After the bout with the migraines, I had learned that I had to lean on God, I had to continue to lay prostrate before him and live for him. I had to continue to have faith and trust in him, that he will heal me from these migraines and my high blood pressure, which was causing the migraines. So, I had to work on my blood pressure in keeping it low and I had to lean not onto my own understanding (Proverbs 3:5).

Talking about God's healing power, let me tell you about my husband. Five months after we got married, my husband had his third stroke. He had two strokes before we got married. The first stroke was when he was forty-two years old. Young, right? Let me tell you how he is blessed just by being connected to me. At this time, my husband just got back into the church, but was not covered by his relationship with God, but mine's. He lost vision in his eye one morning when he had gotten up. He walked to work and said his vision was blurry and then while at work, he called me and said his peripheral vision was completely gone. I told him to go straight to the ER, since he was working at a hospital at the time. Thank God that he was working at the hospital because he probably wouldn't have gone to the hospital and just thought it would blow off. They said he had a stroke in his eye and that he had a blood clot in his head. It wasn't that big and they said it would heal up without surgery because of his young age.

Two years later, he has another stroke while I was with him. He said his arm was numb or falling asleep. I was like, "You need to go to the hospital." He said, "No, I will sleep it off." The next day was Sunday, and we were on our way to church. He could barely walk, take a shower, or get dressed. So I had to help him get dressed. He said he wanted to go to church. I said, "We need to go to the ER, but if you want to go to church, that is where we are going and I will have our pastor pray over you, and then we'll go to the ER." We get to church, I run and get our pastor. The pastor prayed over him and so did the rest of the church. From prayer, we hopped in the car and drove quickly to the hospital with our church nurse following us closely. We get to the hospital and they saw him right away. The nurse said, "You got him here just in time or he could have been paralyzed on one side of his body and would have lost his speech." Lord, I love you! If this isn't a reason to praise the Lord our God, I don't know what will make you praise him! Don't tell me that prayer doesn't change things, because it does!

Then two years after that, he had his third and, hopefully, last stroke. On our first Christmas together as a married couple, he woke up in the middle of the night and started flipping lights on. I was knocked out and was like. "Baby, what's going on?" He said, "My vision is blurry, I can't see." I immediately hopped up, and got dressed, and took him to the hospital. They said he was having another stroke. When I tell you God watches over babies and fools, he was doing just that with him. He will hate me to say that but it's true. We get to the hospital, then he said he was having a real bad headache and started crying because it hurt so badly. Felt like his head was about to explode. He couldn't take it. As we are checking in at the nurse's station, I just held his head and started pleading the blood of Jesus and praying for God's hands to touch him and heal him, and for God to keep him alive as there is work for him to do in this land. The Bible says, if they see the blood, they will pass over you (Exodus 12:13). I felt good and knew that God will take care of him and heal him. God gave me a peace I could not explain. God also has given us the power to lay hands and I had to exercise and apply God's word in that instance (Acts 8:18, Hebrews 6:2, 1 Timothy 4:14, 2 Timothy 1:6).

His blood pressure was so high that he had blood in his brain the size of a golf ball! He was in ICU for six days, then they moved him to a regular room. I felt so sorry for him, to see him this way. He was in so much pain and he was so scared. I have never seen him so scared. So many of my church family members came to see him and prayed for him, including our family and close friends. This made me so happy. Especially, while he was in ICU. When I said we had prayer, the doctors and nurses would wait for us to finish and come in the room and say amen as they were praying with us. You just don't know how much your church family loves and cares for you until they come to visit you or call.

When he was moved to the regular room, he was still not doing well. I prayed every morning when I got to the hospital and every night before I left the hospital. The Bible says, the prayers of the righteous availeth much (James 5:16, Proverbs 16:29). A couple of the deacons came to visit and brighten his day. One of those nights he was in a regular room was New Year's Eve. I stayed until midnight to say Happy New Year, then I went home. He tried to get me to go home before it got too late but I told him I wasn't going home and that we were going to watch our church's watch night service, as this was our first New Year's as Mr. and Mrs. He had occupational therapy and physical therapy. They told him not to go to the bathroom by himself or he may fall. My husband was so determined to go by himself. The nurses told on him when I got to the hospital in the mornings. *Lol!* They kept me posted for sure. They said the quicker he walks up and down the hall on his own, the quicker he will go home. He made sure he was not staying in that hospital past another week. He had enough faith, that he got up every day to walk up and down the hall and even had me watch him. He made sure to report his progress to me before the nurses did. He even was able to start washing himself. I was so proud of him. By the following Sunday, the doctor's released him from the hospital, although they wanted him to go to therapy.

Let me tell you, he refused to go to therapy and was determined to do therapy on his own at home. I stayed home with him for two weeks and during that second week, he told me to go back to work. I said, "Baby, as long as you are here, I'm here to help and assist you with whatever you need." He said back to me that, "I got this!" I said, "Okay, you got this." So I went back to work the following week and checked on him three times a day. He got tired of me checking in on him. When I get home, he's cooking and walking up and down the stairs. He's reading and working on his motor skills with his arms, hands, eyes, and legs. He did this for a month and then he was ready to go back to work. So after his follow up with his doctor and my doctor, they cleared him to go back to work. Determination and faith in God will get you where you need to be (Hebrews 11:1, 3).

CHAPTER 3
Non-Motherhood

The bout with pregnancy. At the age of twenty-one, I had gotten pregnant by someone who knew he was the only one I had been with sexually but would say, "That is not mine," because he did not want to father another child. Can you imagine a man saying that to you when he knows good and well that he is? I was so heartbroken. My co-workers could tell I was hurt. They knew him, as he worked in the store by my job.

Well, I tried on several occasions to talk to him and he did not want to talk to me. My co-workers even tried to talk to him and he was telling them the same thing. It's not his. My co-workers told me to forget him. If he doesn't want the baby, he needs to pay for it. He needs to give you money for an abortion.

I didn't know how to handle this situation. I didn't want to ask him for money. I cried all night and day until I decided to go on and have an abortion. I really didn't want to do this because of my growing up and teachings of God's word, but I called my best friend, scared. She drove me to the clinic to have the procedure done. I'm still crying because I did the ultimate thing I was raised to not do and that was to kill my unborn child. I had asked God for forgiveness but it haunted me for years.

I went on with my life and about thirteen years later, I get pregnant again at the age of thirty-four. This time, I wanted to keep it, but the guy I was dealing with at this time said to me, "If you have this baby, I will fight for custody," and I didn't want that because at this time, I had lost my job and just started my master's degree program. So he said he would pay for the abortion. I was like, "No! I can't do this again, I must have this baby." I can't go through the pain of another abortion. I was so stressed and mad that I lost my baby. My stomach was hurting to no intent while at the mall. I went to the bathroom and I was bleeding profusely. I hurried home and had to go to the bathroom again and next thing I see is my baby fetus in the toilet. That's all I needed.

Once again, I'm crying and all bent over. Don't know what to do, but pray to God. He has helped me thus far. I ask, "Why me, Lord?" I promised not to have another abortion. Why couldn't this one live? I just wanted to be married when I had gotten pregnant again. So, this haunts me more, because I have seen the fetus's eyes, head, arms, legs, hands, and feet. It was a part of me. I was eight weeks pregnant at the time this had happened. I had just started graduate school and just lost my good government job of sixteen years. I had a lot on my shoulders. I didn't know if I could go on in life. Even wondering how I was going to take care of the child on my own. This one really hurts inside. Then, a small voice said to me, "I don't put more on you than you can bear." At that time, I promised myself that I would stay on the path of righteousness, this time, for his name's sake and not fall astray.

After this, I did not want to talk to anyone, not even my best friend. I didn't talk to her for months. I even didn't feel like going to church. I totally isolated myself from the world. I felt really bad and didn't think that God would forgive me for what I have done. I sinned against him and my body. As the scriptures says, your bodies are the temples of the Holy Ghost (1 Corinthians 6:19). So I defiled my body. Spirits are real and do transfer from person to person, but I am a believer and witness that if you keep your mind on Christ, he will keep you in perfect peace (Isaiah 26:3). If you continue to seek his face daily (1Chronicles 16:11, 2 Chronicles 7:14, and Psalms 105:4), God will prevail in your life. From this time forward, I had guarded my life behind going to church and being more involved in my sorority to keep me busy and my mind off of being lonely. I had also started getting serious about my career and making more money and spending more time with my family. I did all of this to keep my mind off of not being a mother and not having any children of my own. I really did want to have children and still do. This had bothered me a lot every time someone mention they were pregnant or when someone asks when I will have one, but I have come to a point in my life that what God has for me, it is for me. Don't get me wrong because I was happy for whoever had gotten pregnant and I always supported them, wishing it was me. I just need to enjoy God. He is my fortress and my redeemer. In him will I trust, move, and have my being.

I couldn't have any children then, but little did I know later down the line, he will bless me with four step-children, three of whom I have a good relationship with, but I still wanted one of my own. So, I tried several times to get pregnant the regular way. Of course, nothing happens. Then my doctor suggested that I go to a fertility clinic to see what my options would be and handed me a pamphlet of one of the facilities suggested. After looking at costs and looking at my health insurance, my health insurance would not cover the costs of the process and procedures. So, I just gave up hope of having children because I couldn't even afford the process and procedure to go through with it and to even see if I was fertile at this late age in life. Then things just went downhill from there. I started having woman issues and having cycles from twenty-eight days to twenty-one days, to sixty days, to fifty days, then back to twenty-one day and twenty-eight day cycles. This went on for three years. Then all of a sudden, no cycle for months the year I turn fifty. So, then I just said forget it. It just isn't for me. I really went through a mental stability of ups and downs to nights crying because I felt that God was displeased with me for what happened earlier in life.

One night in my crying and praying to God, I listened and knew it was him. He said to me, "You must forgive yourself. You have forgiven everyone else, but yourself. You think having a child will make you whole, but I make you whole, I fill that void, have you forgotten? You must pick up your cross and live for me (Jesus that is), live for your husband and family that I gave to you. Fulfill your purpose in life. Tell your story. No one can tell it, but you. You will heal from this outpouring of your life for the world to see." I tell you, when God spoke, he spoke and once again, I had to do what he tells me to do, so I can be blessed. Who doesn't want to be blessed by God? No one, I hope. Through this whole ordeal, God took care of my needs and doubled up on what I should have had in the beginning. Only God's grace and mercy is what kept my spirits lifted up through this whole ordeal. It wasn't what I had planned, but God's plan is not our plans and his ways are past finding out.

CHAPTER 4
Career Life

For God's continued love for me, he let me suffer (Acts 9:16). That year of the loss of my baby started off with the loss of my federal government job. I was forced to resign my position with the federal government because of someone in the office being jealous of me and another co-worker. So they tried to ping me on using my federal government credit card for personal use, which I had paid back and did not charge over $800. They made me feel like a suspect, but in fact, I was the victim. They saw me being successful and not a dummy. I was learning faster and more than they were. From that day on, I did not know how I was going to make ends meet. I lived in my apartment for two months without paying the rent. Stayed as long as I could. Then eventually, I had to give in and move back in with my parents after four years of being by myself until I could get back on my feet. This was an adjustment.

I started going to the library every day to search for jobs. I started praying every day, asking God to bless me with a job. I was also fasting intermittently, without knowing, because I didn't have money to eat with. I only ate dinner. I did that for two months until I landed a temporary job with a temp company. I had several temp jobs until November of that year. While I was working those temporary jobs, all of my money went to my parents to help with bills in the house and to getting my medicine as I did not have health insurance during that time. I was really struggling and didn't want anyone to know that I was. I felt my parents didn't care if I was struggling, just that they needed my money to keep a roof over their heads and the lights on. We had no A/C in the summer time and no heat in the winter. I might as well had just be living on the streets, is how I felt, but I had moved my one-bedroom apartment into their house so I might as well stay. My parents didn't want anyone to know they were struggling as well, but don't drain your child's funds when they didn't ask to be brought in this world. Though the Bible says honor thy parents (Exodus 20:12, Deuteronomy 5:16, Matthew 19:19, Mark 7:10), I did just that and kept it moving, but I had made myself a crutch for them in the meantime. This is not what God wants us to be and that is a hindrance, a crutch or an enabler. I won't go further into it. All I can say is, "But God!"

So, one of the temp jobs became permanent. I stayed there for two years only because God did not want me to be flat broke, but wanted me to have some money coming in. I found work near where my school was located, so I could finish my master's degree in Human Resources Management. This is where God would let me take stair steps to success. I'm telling you, when you put your whole heart, mind, and soul into God, he will bless you to no end! Just start living for Christ! You will see.

Five months after I received my master's degree, a lady called about a contract job doing work I used to do in the federal government. I saw this as a shoe in the door to being a Fed again! So, I took that job, worked there for eight months. During that time, I didn't make much and my commute was four hours a day. Paying to get to work was taking up most of my money. If I took off, I did not get paid. I was like, "Lord, I'm not used to this," but I knew this was a sacrifice I had to make. Then I get word the contract was lost and I have to find a new job by December of that year, after only being at this job for seven months. The contract was sold in July. So after the news in July, I get a call from another contracting company the following week, asking me to send my resume to them. Then the contracting company tells me not to go to the job fair that was going on, so they would not have competition and that I was a shoo-in with them. So, without using my better judgment, I didn't go to the job fair. Then a month later, I get a call from that particular contracting company asking me what salary am I asking for or looking for. I told them and just a few hours later, they called back and said I got the job on the new contract! Look at God!

Three weeks later, I started at the new company and was one of the first persons on the new contract. I had my ups and downs on this job, but I had actually liked contracting for a particular federal government agency, even though it started getting stressful. I felt it was about time to start looking for another job after a year of being there. I applied for a job at one of my old agencies in 2009. Interviewed there and was selected for the position. Once selected, I had to go through the security clearance trying to get a secret clearance. So, I filled out the fifty-page paperwork and returned it to the agency by the due date. After a month or two went by, the agency contacted me and told me that they could not hire me because of my background and credit. I never heard of such a thing, but I didn't worry about it and said I'll try again in 2015. Maybe all the things in my security file will have been deleted because after ten years, your credit and file should be cleared up. This was a heartbreaker and thought I would never get back into the government. But God told me to wait (Psalms 27:14), so I just waited until the time was right.

Well, I ended up staying on that contract for eight years. The contract is about to end and is up for bids and this time, I said I needed to get back in the government so I can still retire early if I wanted to. So I started applying for federal jobs. I had interviewed with three different agencies. The one I really wanted, I prayed every day for that job after I applied for it. Took the job announcement to church and took it to the altar and prayed over it. I said, "Lord, if this is for me, it is for me." I went in for the interview and knocked the interview out of the park. I was confident in every answer I had given. I got a call on the Monday after the interview saying I was selected for the position! Then I had to go through the clearance process. I was like, "My God!" This is what I dreaded because my credit was jacked up, but I have been through this before in 2009 after being selected for another federal government position. God spoke to me and said that I had to remember to ask questions when I didn't understand, to do what is asked of me, and not assume the worse. So they had questions about my credit and I answered them with a letter of response to each item thoroughly and to show I was paying the bills or they have been taken care of. If I didn't go through what I went through before and God telling me to just do what was asked, that I will get through the background check and get the job. So a month later, I get the call that I have been cleared to work and when I can start. I was so excited, I couldn't wait. Back being a government employee.

Let me tell you, right before I applied to that job, I did a vision board. I also vowed to the Lord, that I would be faithful in my tithe giving. For the Bible says, "Bring ye all the tithes into the storehouse, that there may be meat in mine house, and prove me now herewith, saith the Lord of hosts, if I will not open you the windows of heaven, and pour you out a blessing, that there shall not be room enough to receive it" (2 Chronicles 3:8). Who doesn't want to receive an overflowing of blessings from the Lord thy God? Just don't tithe for the blessings, tithe because it pleases God. If you do it to please him, he will bless you even more abundantly.

On that vision board, I put a vision of me getting back in the government and my three-year plan to be a GS-13 and becoming a Team Lead within that three-year plan. Well I was at that agency for three years and within that time, I got promoted every year until I became a GS-13. Two months after I became a GS-13, I started applying for team lead positions at the agency I was currently in and several other agencies. Once again, I had three interviews lined up. The third one was by surprise and that surprise interview landed me a team lead position with another federal agency. Once again, after I applied for the jobs, I took all three to the altar this time and said, "God, let thy will be done. Wherever you think I need to be, that's what I want." I also told him which job I thought suits me better. God ended up giving me that job and I've been there ever since. To say all of this, goes back to God's word where it says write the vision and make it plain (Habakkuk 2:2)! That's all I did! I wrote the vision and made it plain. It's in his word! If this doesn't make you a believer, I don't know what will. Just applying God's word in your life makes all the difference.

CHAPTER 5
The Dating Game and Marriage

Regarding getting married for those who desire to be married. I had always wanted to be married. I had put this vision on that vision board—that I was going to get married to the guy I was currently dating. A month later, he proposed to me and nine months later, we got married! Who would have thought? We are still together after four years of marriage and nine years of togetherness!

Let me tell you, this was a journey. I had always wanted to be married ever since I was in my twenties. I have been in several relationships in which I thought the man I was dating at that time was the one. With that said, God never told me any of them was the one I was supposed to marry, but he reminded me that "he that finds a wife, finds a good thing," not *she* who finds a husband, finds a good thing (Proverbs 18:22). So, I was going about it wrong from the time I was twenty-five years old. I say twenty-five because I wasn't looking to be with any man before that age. Every guy I dated before the age of twenty-five, I didn't look for them. They actually sought me out and asked me to date them. Little did I know then that one of them would be the one I end up with in the end. Even till this day, the ones I did not end up with check in every now and then to see how I'm doing, but I know they call because they know they messed up and could have had a good thing. For in the Bible, it states that, "no good thing is withheld from them that walk uprightly" (Psalms 84:11). *Lol!* That went for me too. I wasn't walking uprightly with the Lord. That's why I couldn't withhold a good thing or a good man, in my eyes.

One guy I was dating after the age of twenty-five, he had it going on ladies. He had a good paying job, his own house, and two cars, and never asked me to pay for anything.

He was respectful to my parents and to his own parents. He took me out of town with him on business trips, homecoming games in North Carolina, and NFL games down in Charlotte, to see the Carolina Panthers and even his team the Cowboys when they played the Panthers in a playoff game. The Panthers beat them badly. *Lol!* It was great to see and cheer the Panthers on, since I'm a diehard Washington Redskins fan. His parents would even meet us at the games, as they are diehard Panthers fans. I thought all was good until he went on vacation and did not take me but instead went with his best friend, who is a female by the way. I didn't know how to take that. He was like, "She's my best friend and you should understand that," but I didn't. So I let him go. We kept in touch and saw each other on and off for some years, I didn't know really how to let him go. Well God made sure I would let him go by finding out he was getting married, just five months after our last break up and that last break up, he left me. My feelings were so hurt. I found out through a mutual friend that he was getting married to some lady that he was dating for a few years, hmm, while we were dating, but I digress, because we were on and off and I was dating other men as well. Then it was confirmed a month later, after that and one of my other girlfriends found his registry and the date they were getting married. I was wondering if he was going to tell me and he never did. He did the "okie doke" and said I left my camera at his house and his father was going to bring my camera to me because he was on vacation. His vacation ended up being his honeymoon. Can you feel my pain? I was done and I mean done with him at this point.

Then there was another young man that I dealt with in my late twenties, I believe I was twenty-nine at the time. This guy was a smooth operator. We worked in the same building, but not for the same company. He was a smoker, I have asthma. How was that going to work? We hung out literally almost every day after work. I either went to his house or he came to mine. He had multiple streams of income, so he had money in his pocket. He never asked me to come out of my pocket for anything. He took me out of town with his family to Las Vegas and he came with me and my family on our first family cruise. On that cruise is when it all started to go downhill. I have a smart mouth, I know, and because of the first guy I talked about, I had trust issues and that's what started our arguments. This guy even bought me two rings on the trip. One was a pearl ring and the other was a pre-engagement ring. Thank God it was a pre-engagement ring. To me it didn't mean anything. I was like thanks, but he wanted to show it off. Bad idea. Not too long after that, we kept having arguments and one day we argued so much, we were at a barbershop and I was getting sleepy and I was ready to go home, but my car was at his house. So, I just went outside and waited. He came outside and started yelling and I'm yelling back. Then we get in the car and started yelling again. He started driving and told me to get out the car. I said no, then he stops the car, comes to the other side, and drags me out of the car, and throws me to the ground. Then I got up and started screaming, and hollering, and kicking, and punching, so we are now fighting in front of the barbershop. He punched me in the mouth and busted my lip. Needless to say, that was the end of that relationship. I got to work the next day and they had to put him in another building. This fight wasn't my first rodeo, as the man I married, was my first boyfriend after high school and him and I had fought a few times but they were all started by me. I swung first and let him tell it, I beat him up, but I was the one with the black eye. This incident though was not the case. This man was malicious and did not have to put his hands on me. He was also a friend of my cousin's cousin, whose barbershop we were fighting in front of. Needless to say, after that, they weren't close friends anymore. I was embarrassed for a while about this incident because we worked in the same building, but my co-workers made sure I did not feel that way. My co-workers were my support system and my bodyguards until his company had moved him to another location. At this point, yes, I am thanking God that nothing worst happened to me besides a busted lip, because it could have been worst.

From there, my self-esteem was pretty low, but I got back on my feet and started dating again a couple of years later. I started seeing someone I knew since elementary school. I had really liked him but he ended up being a functioning alcoholic. You could smell the alcohol just reaping through his pores and his breath! My God! I couldn't even think to kiss him. This was a turn off for sure. Needless to say, this did not last long. He's a very good person, has a degree, a good job, his own home, and a car. He had all of that and it was just not good enough for me to stay. I learned that lesson already.

Because of the low self-esteem, I let this happen. A married man started to chase me until I gave in. Then his wife left him when she found out he was chasing me and hanging out in the streets and clubs. He was cool, but he didn't have the money to take care of me; his wife did. He was confident enough to admit it and that I can respect, but he didn't want to leave her because she had money. She told me I wasn't the reason she left. She added that I was just the topping on the cake. She had several reasons. I felt bad and apologized to her because I didn't want that on my conscience and I wanted to be able to get married and not have my spouse do the same thing, as the Bible says, you reap what you sow. I also had to repent to God and boy, did I lay prostrate before him with this one. I was not sowing correctly at this point, but I also wasn't looking to be with him in a relationship and him vice versa. He was just chasing me for the thrill to see if he could get away with it and he didn't. See how God don't like ugly? He thought he could do his thing and still be with his wife, but God said no. Then when she kicked him out, he wants to be with me. I decided to give it a try since he's not with his wife any longer. So he takes me to Miami and several other cities nearby for short weekend getaways. Then I get pregnant, as I mentioned in chapter 2. This was the baby I had lost. So you can see how this ended. He thought if I had the baby, he could take it and get back with his wife so they could raise my child as a family, since I wasn't trying to have the abortion. This really stressed me out. I was not having another woman raise my child. My blood pressure had gotten so high and I was stressed to no end, I lost the baby. At this point, I never asked God what I was doing wrong. I would just ask, "Why me?"

So you can see I was not waiting on God to move. I was yet hopping into another relationship. Started dating someone else I have known for years, but how well did I know him? He caught me in a vulnerable state. He was living with someone else while seeing me and told me she was leaving to go be with her fiancé and that her parents set up the marriage. Lo and behold, he was still seeing her, as they had gotten into a fight in front of their apartment. I don't know why I was dragged into this drama. Two months later, I was at his place and the cops came to get him because she had pictures of her all bloody with swollen lips and eyes. I was like, again, "Why me, Lord?" This man told me he wanted to marry me and then told me to set a date and look for a venue. Mind you, he had been married before so we wouldn't be able to get married at church and that is not what I wanted. This was my sign that I should leave this one alone. He understood, so we are still cordial with each other and I know he would have my back at any time.

A couple of years later, I thought that was enough time to start dating again. This time, the guy who asked me out was someone I met on a bus coming home from work one evening. To find out this guy has three children, one step-son, and an ex-wife. My God! Why didn't I run? I dealt with him for a year, but I shouldn't have, if I didn't want to marry someone that had been married before. What was I thinking? We had our issues. Me feeling he still had a sexual relationship with his ex-wife or him still wanting to be with her, because she is the mother of two of his three children. Then I had to deal with a jealous son that thought I was taking his father away from him and I wasn't trying to deal with all of that, but was dealing with it somehow. Until, enough was enough and the guy I was dealing with was letting his young kids watch adult cartoons and he didn't have a problem with it. I was like, dude, this is not healthy for them. These cartoons are showing naked people, having blood all over the place. He said they've seen worse or will see worse and if he's watching it with him, it's okay. I was like not while I'm around. Then his son was disrespectful, I called him out on it and then the fella I was dating said I should not have corrected his child. I told him, if we are together as a couple, he needs to respect his elders and you should allow me to correct him verbally. It was me or the children. I didn't want to make him choose, so I left. He wanted to make up and take me out for my birthday. He went out of town on my birthday and didn't come back in town until that Sunday. I was so done that day because I was with my sorors getting pedicures after chapter meeting. My heart was so broken at that point that I started tearing up. My sorors came to the rescue and we went out to dinner for my birthday that night to get my mind off of it. I will never forget that. Those young ladies are still my friends to this day. This was the last straw, so I left this one alone. Just told him that I can't deal with the disappearing acts and the fighting with his son for his attention anymore. He understood and we parted ways on a good note.

Little did I know, all of this was setting me up for that final rodeo with dating. I had actually started to give up on dating because I was getting to old to get married and too old to have children. I had turned forty and being single and forty to me, was a "no-no." I was starting to be called names like an old maid and told I will never have any children. The good part is that God kept me sane after all of this. Never at one time was I jealous of any of my friends who have children or have gotten married. So, I decided to just continue to live my life for Christ and continue to just date socially, and not get into a relationship, and actually not look for the man. Even though I wasn't looking in the first place, I just didn't want to be alone. That was my issue.

But God! Can I say this again? But God! While I was just minding my business, my career life was moving steady, continuing to pray, and fast, and gaining a closer relationship with Christ, my "now" husband comes. At this time we were just friends, then he came to my house just to see me and let me know he was back in the city after being away for some years. We kept in touch after that and just talked on the phone, until one day he invited me over to do a tasting. He said he was working on his skills in the kitchen because he is a chef. He invited me several times before but I never had time to until this time. He has been back home for three years at this point. Then four months later, we decided to start dating exclusively, again.

We had our ups and downs. We even broke up the relationship twice in our five years of dating. That second breakup, I laid it before the Lord. He told me to just wait and see what will happen. Continue to be yourself and we will see. So at this point, I had to trust God. I told him, "Okay, I'll do what you ask me to do." This is when I learned to just do what he asks me to do and he will provide. I even talked to my pastor about this on more than one occasion and he told me, "Your boy will be back, just watch, he isn't going far, he loves you and so do I. I'm not going to stir you wrong. You're my sister first, so you know I will hurt him, if he hurts you." *Lol!* The second time around, I was a little smarter and so was he. It took me a minute, but I had to stop my communication with him. I was doing my thing and he was doing his. I haven't had communication with him in two months, then all of a sudden, after seeing me at a gathering, he contacted me and said how he misses me. We talked and laid some ground rules and decided to give it one more try.

For a year, I would always tell him we need to go to a counselor that is married to tell us what we are doing wrong and to tell us how to make our relationship better. So, after almost a year of begging him to go to a counselor, he came out to say that if I want to do this, I have to find the counselor. So I did some research and found a Christian counselor in our area. We went to the counselor for eight weeks and received a certificate for finishing the counseling. It was an awakening, as a lot of things I went through were because of my past relationships, not trusting anyone, and when I was raped as a young girl. I had to get that out. I still have some issues today but with the help of my husband, I am breaking through. Well, a month after the counseling, my husband proposed to me right after church one Sunday in November, when our Bishop had come out from being bedridden and gave the Word that day. My husband felt convicted by the Word and said he needed to stop procrastinating and take me as his wife. I was in total shock. So, I didn't want to tell anyone until he actually put a ring on it. He put a ring on it two months later. Once he did that, I went to my pastor for his blessings. He had nothing bad to say. He just wanted me to make sure if this is what I wanted, he'll have my back either way. He just wanted the best for me and for me to be happy. I told him I was happy. Then six months later, we confessed our love for one another and made a covenant with God, till death do we part in front of 250 people. This is the best decision I have made in my entire life. That year was even the best year of my life. My husband is my best friend, my confidant, my support system, my laughing partner, business partner, and I can go on and on.

What I can say is God is not a genie, but he will give you the desires of your heart… just keep your mind on him. I'm telling you, God will turn your life around when you start depending on him and take yourself out of it! Just put your faith and trust in God! I was too busy trying to take care of things myself instead of consulting him first. Not asking if whatever I am doing is what he wants me to do or to happen in my life. Then when

I had consulted him, I had to trust that he would get it done. The Bible says, "But seek ye first the kingdom of God, and his righteousness; and all these things shall be added unto you" (Matthew 6:33). With this said, we all should be doing this in all things that we do. We should go to God first, before even making a move. God will give you the guidance and steps to take to get it done. He will also provide you the things needed to get it done as well. Think on all these things that I have been through. When I went to God in prayer is when he supplied me with all my needs and when I did what he said, he gave me the desires of my heart.

> *But they that wait on the Lord shall renew their strength; they shall mount up with wings as eagles; they shall run, and not be weary, and they shall walk, and not faint. (Isaiah 40:31)*

ABOUT THE AUTHOR

Wanda Bright is a native of Washington, DC. She was born and raised in the District of Columbia. She is a graduate of Calvin Coolidge Senior High School. She is a graduate of the University of the District of Columbia, where she received a BBA degree in Business Administration. She also received an MBA degree in Human Resources Management.

Wanda is a member of Alpha Kappa Alpha Sorority, Incorporated, and a member of the National Association for the Advancement of Colored People. Wanda is a member of both Calvin Coolidge Senior High School and University of the District of Columbia's Alumni Associations. Wanda is also a lifetime member of The First United Church of Jesus Christ (Apostolic) in Washington, DC, also known as the "Church of Champions" where she is a member of several ministries.

Wanda is part owner of Bright on Thyme Catering with her husband, who is the chef extraordinaire. She also owns her own HR and Financial Consulting business, along with owning a travel business.

For speaking engagements, HR and financial consulting, booking travel and book signings go to www.wandahaynesbright.com

CPSIA information can be obtained
at www.ICGtesting.com
Printed in the USA
BVHW070849101121
621186BV00003B/221